Historical Biographies

AGATHA CHRISTIE

Detective Novelist and Playwright

by Grace Hansen

DiscoverRoo
An Imprint of Pop!
popbooksonline.com

WELCOME TO DiscoverRoo!

This book is filled with videos, puzzles, games, and more! Scan the QR codes* while you read, or visit the website below to make this book pop.

https://popbooksonline.com/christie

abdobooks.com
Published by Pop!, a division of ABDO, PO Box 398166, Minneapolis, Minnesota 55439.

Printed in the United States of America, North Mankato, Minnesota.

102022
012023

THIS BOOK CONTAINS RECYCLED MATERIALS

Cover Photo: Getty Images; Shutterstock Images
Interior Photos: Getty Image Collection; Shutterstock Images; AP Images; Alamy
Editor: Elizabeth Andrews
Series Designers: Laura Graphenteen; Neil Klinepier

Library of Congress Control Number: 2022941239

Publisher's Cataloging-in-Publication Data

Names: Hansen, Grace, author.
Title: Agatha Christie: detective novelist and playwright / by Grace Hansen
Description: Minneapolis, Minnesota : Pop!, 2023 | Series: Historical biographies | Includes online resources and index.
Identifiers: ISBN 9781098243388 (lib. bdg.) | ISBN 9781098244088 (ebook)
Subjects: LCSH: Mallowan, Agatha Christie, 1890-1976--Juvenile literature. | Authors, English--Biography--Juvenile literature. | Women authors--Biography--Juvenile literature. | Detective and mystery stories, English--Juvenile literature. | Playwrights--Biography--Juvenile literature.
Classification: DDC 823.912 [B]--dc23

*Scanning QR codes requires a web-enabled smart device with a QR code reader app and a camera.

TABLE OF CONTENTS

CHAPTER 1

YOUNG AGATHA

The seaside town of Torquay in Devon, England, has been the birthplace of some impressive people. From explorers and **archaeologists** to cinematographers and actors, the talent to come from this tiny town seems boundless. But the most

WATCH A VIDEO HERE!

notable character from Torquay may just be best-selling crime novelist Agatha Christie.

Devon inspired the settings in some of Christie’s works, including And Then There Were None.

She was born Agatha Mary Clarissa Miller on September 15, 1890. Agatha grew up in a well-to-do family. Her father, Fredrick, homeschooled her. Her mother, Clara, told her **captivating** stories.

Today, Torquay is home to about 65,000 people. It is known for its beautiful weather.

Agatha's parents decided she could wait until the age of eight to learn to read. But Agatha taught herself before her fifth birthday!

This oil painting, titled Lost in Reverie, *by Douglas John Connah shows Christie at age four.*

Young Agatha enjoyed reading, writing, and math. She liked to dance. She played piano and the **mandolin**. She had real friends and imaginary ones. In her later years, Agatha looked back on her life fondly and said, "One of the luckiest things that can happen to you in life is, I think, to have a happy childhood. I had a very happy childhood."

DID YOU KNOW?

Agatha studied classical music in Paris in her late teens. However, she was too shy to perform in front of people.

CHAPTER 2

CAST OF CHARACTERS

Agatha's creativity was blossoming by the age of 18. She had written short stories and even a novel. But after several publishers declined to work with her, a writing career was far off. So, Agatha distracted herself with activities like hunting, horseback riding, and parties. In the fall of

LEARN MORE HERE!

1912, at one of those parties, Agatha met Archibald "Archie" Christie. Archie would become a pilot in the British Army. The two married in 1914, before Archie went to serve in World War I (1914-1918).

Christie was always imagining up something new.

RECURRING ROLES

Christie created two equally famous characters: detectives Hercule Poirot and Miss Marple. Jane Marple was the protagonist in 12 Christie novels. Her first appearance came in the short story "The Tuesday Night Club" (1927). Both characters have been portrayed by several actors on stage and on screen.

Agatha worked as a nurse while Archie was away. But she also wrote. In 1916, she finished her first published novel *The Mysterious Affair at Styles* (1920). Agatha sent the **manuscript** to several publishing houses. Finally, The Bodley Head agreed. The story's main character, Hercule Poirot, was inspired by the Belgian soldiers and refugees Agatha met during the war. Poirot would become one of Christie's most well-known characters. The short, **intense** Belgian detective would go on to appear in 33 novels, two plays, and more than 50 short stories. The most notable include *Murder on the Orient Express* (1933) and *Death on the Nile* (1937).

The first film based on the novel Murder on the Orient Express *was released in 1974.*

CHAPTER 3

STRANGER THAN FICTION

The year 1926 brought great change for Agatha. She and Archie purchased a large and lovely home in Sunningdale early in the year. Archie had left the army and was on his way to becoming a successful businessman. In April, Agatha's mother died. The loss took a toll on Agatha. She spent months cleaning out her childhood home. During this

Christie managed to write works she was proud of during difficult times.

difficult time, Agatha's novel *The Murder of Roger Ackroyd* was published. It was the third book to feature Poirot and was also said to be one of the author's favorite works.

When Agatha returned to Sunningdale in August, Archie admitted to being in love with a friend of the family. He asked for a divorce, which upset her further. Agatha's sadness grew through the Autumn. On December 3, Agatha drove away. Her car was found abandoned the next morning.

The author's mysterious disappearance became a big news story. It even made the front page of *The New York Times*. Search parties that included more than 1,000 police officers and 15,000 volunteers scoured England. The case was finally cracked ten days later. More than 200 miles (365km) north of her home, staff at the Swan Hydropathic Hotel recognized Agatha. She had checked in under a different name. When Archie came to retrieve her, Agatha did not recognize him. She also could not remember the events of the prior weeks.

Christie's breakdown was followed closely by the press.

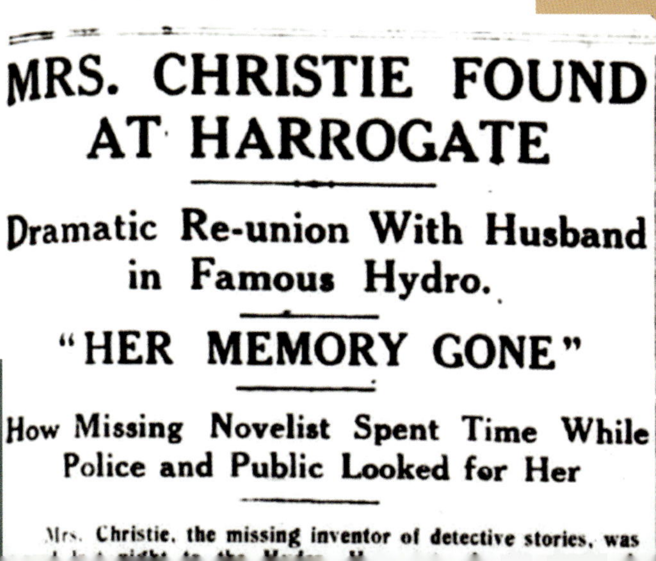
MRS. CHRISTIE FOUND AT HARROGATE

Dramatic Re-union With Husband in Famous Hydro.

"HER MEMORY GONE"

How Missing Novelist Spent Time While Police and Public Looked for Her

Mrs. Christie, the missing inventor of detective stories, was

CHAPTER 4

A NEW NARRATIVE

Agatha, broken and at her lowest, went to live with her sister. She also started seeing a **psychiatrist** for help. In 1928, she divorced Archie. The same year *The Mystery of the Blue Train* was published. The novel again starred Hercule Poirot and was one she'd written during the hardest time in her life.

COMPLETE AN ACTIVITY HERE!

Agatha and her second husband, Max Mallowan, posing near their holiday home in Devon, which she described as "the loveliest place in the world."

Christie enjoyed traveling to wonderful places in her later years, like the Acropolis in Athens, Greece, in the summer of 1958.

In the fall, Agatha realized one of her greatest dreams. She traveled on the Orient Express to Istanbul, Turkey, and then Baghdad, Iraq. It was in Iraq that she met **archaeologists** Leonard and Katharine Woolley. They invited her to return for their next dig in February of 1930. On that trip, Agatha met and fell in love with archaeologist Max Mallowan. The two married that September. These exciting and adventurous times inspired *Murder on the Orient Express*.

Agatha and Max had a well-balanced life. Between travel and dig sites, the couple enjoyed quiet time at their countryside home and with family. During World War II (1939-1945) Agatha stayed in England while Max worked in Cairo, Egypt. Through the war years, Agatha published an amazing 13 works. One of

"I think the real work [in writing] is done in thinking out the development of your story and worrying about it until it comes right. That may take quite a while. Then, when you've got all your material together, all that remains is to find time to write the thing."

And Then There Were None has sold more than 100 million copies.

those became the world's best-selling mystery novel of all time, *And Then There Were None.* Christie would later say of the work, "I don't say it is the play or book of mine that I like best, or even that I think it is my best, but I do think … it is a better piece of craftsmanship than anything else I have written."

CHAPTER 5

A RECORD-BREAKING LIFE

Agatha was not finished making history. On October 6, 1952, Christie's play *The Mousetrap* debuted at the Theatre Royal in Nottingham. The show never stopped. In 2022, with more than 28,500 performances given, the beloved **whodunit** was still running after 70 years.

EXPLORE LINKS HERE!

The Mousetrap has an exciting twist ending that playgoers are asked not to reveal!

Agatha authored into her later years, but at a much slower pace. After feverishly writing more than 70 novels, dozens of short stories, 16 plays, two autobiographies, and poems, the author had earned a rest. On January 12, 1976, Agatha Christie died peacefully at her home in Winterbrook.

Agatha left quite the legacy. Her published works have been translated

A memorial honoring Christie stands in the heart of London's theater district.

into more than 100 languages with over two billion copies sold. Agatha's beloved characters have leaped off the pages and onto the stage and big screen. With murder mystery fans around the globe, Agatha Christie will go down in history as one of the most **prolific** writers of fiction.

MARY WESTMACOTT

Christie wrote six non-murder mystery novels under the pen name Mary Westmacott. The timing of the genre and persona change came at a very interesting time. Westmacott's first book, a tragedy called *Giant's Bread*, was written in 1928 after Christie's life had been turned upside down.

IMPORTANT DATES

SEPTEMBER 15, 1890

Agatha Mary Clarissa Miller is born in Torquay, Devon, England.

JANUARY 1, 1917

Christie completes her first novel, *The Mysterious Affair at Styles*. After being denied by six publishers, The Bodley Head accepts the title three years later.

JANUARY 1, 1934

Murder on the Orient Express is published.

NOVEMBER 6, 1939

And Then There Were None is published.

JANUARY 12, 1976

Christie dies peacefully at home at the age of 85.

OCTOBER 6, 1952

The Mousetrap, a murder mystery play, premiers at the Theatre Royal in Nottingham, England.

MAKING CONNECTIONS

TEXT-TO-SELF

Do you enjoy mystery stories? Why or why not?

TEXT-TO-TEXT

Have you read any other books about the life of an author? How were their lives different from or similar to Agatha Christie's?

TEXT-TO-WORLD

Why do you think crime and mystery novels are so popular among people around the world?

GLOSSARY

archaeologist — a scientist who works in the field of archaeology, the study of past human life and culture.

captivating — causing one to be charmed or fascinated.

intense — having or showing strong feelings or opinions; extremely serious.

mandolin — a musical instrument in the lute family with four to six pairs of strings that are usually strummed.

manuscript — a piece of writing prepared by the author before it becomes a printed book.

prolific — creating new works or ideas in abundance; productive.

psychiatrist — a medical doctor who treats people with mental and emotional illnesses.

whodunit — a fictional crime story, in which the object is usually to discover who has done or committed the crime.

INDEX

DiscoverRoo!
ONLINE RESOURCES

This book is filled with videos, puzzles, games, and more! Scan the QR codes* while you read, or visit the website below to make this book pop.

https://popbooksonline.com/christie

*Scanning QR codes requires a web-enabled smart device with a QR code reader app and a camera.